RUNNERS ON THE SOUL

by Sean Haughton

A Collection of Dark Short Stories

Runners On The Soul

RUNNERS ON THE SOUL

SEAN HAUGHTON

Copyright © 2023, 2024 by Sean Haughton

Second Edition

First published in 2023. This edition first published in 2024.

All rights reserved. No part of this book may be reproduced or used in any manner without the express written permission of the publisher except for the use of brief quotations in a book review.

Sean Haughton has asserted the moral right to be identified as the author of this work in accordance with the Copyright, Designs & Patents Act 1988.

Cover art & design courtesy of the creation tools of Canva.

Reader discretion may be advised.

ISBN: 978-1-9162751-9-5

It's not only my dreams; my belief is that all these dreams are yours as well...

WERNER HERZOG

CONTENTS

PREFACE	i
WHAT'S IT ALL ABOUT?	1
SOMEWHERE IN THE DEPTHS	4
DREAMS	5
MONKEY TALES	8
NOT A CHANCE WAS STOOD	11
MORNING, MR. MAGPIE	12
BOOKSHELF MUSINGS	13
EIGHT STEP	14
THE INITIAL CODE	16
THE SIBLING GAME	20
LIFE'S TRUTHS AND CRIMES	21
RIVERS, LIKE POETIC SPEECHES	22
THE PARK	24
SEPTEMBER 18TH	25
HORROR, STRIFE, MANIA, ANXIETY	26
"WALL"	27
AT LEAST YOUR SONG IS PLAYING	28
TOUCHED BY FLAMES	29
KHARMIC CONSEQUENCES	31
VALENTINE & POE	34
GOLDEN HEEL	35
THURSDAY MORNING JOURNEY	36
A DEADPAN NOTE	39
THE KING	40
EVERY ONCE IN A WHILE…	41
LOST MOMENTS?	42
THREE LINE WHIP	43

A BRANCH	44
THE LOST WOMAN	45
TRANQUIL IS THE STREAM	46
FAREWELL TO THE POSSESSIONS	47
TODAY IT WAS CLEAR	48
02:03	50
TT-MH	52
THE FALLING CURTAIN	54
NIGHTHAWK	55
SEPTEMBER, 15TH	57
WORDS WITH A LADY OF GOD	58
ATONEMENT & FAITH	60
TAKE, SEEK, FIND	61
HAS IT BEGUN?	62
POISONOUS REFLECTIONS	63
DESTITUTE DREAMS	64
REFLECTING ON A WORK	65
NOT EVEN HERE	67
SCARS FROM THE CROWN	68
MISGUIDED CALLINGS	69
MONDAY, 5TH	70
DON'T GIVE UP	71
R2	72
A STORY ENDS AND A STORY BEGINS	73
COLD REVELATONS	74
IDEATION vs. FEAR	75
THE SPARK OF LIFE	77
A CREATIVE MAN'S BURDEN	78
A TINY TRAGEDY	80
PAUSING AGAIN	81

BOUNCING OFF THE WALLS	84
AIR	86
HE'S LONG FORGOTTEN	87
SAME OLD	88
A STORY OF MEN	89
A TUB OF HUMAN WINE	90
DISORDERLY	92
AND YET...	93
WE?	95
DARK AURAS	96
I WALKED, AND I WALK	98
BUT...	103
I WALKED, IN THE EVENINGS	105
CONTRADICTORY ANECODTES ON A LOST "LOVE"	106
A WOMAN I NEVER KNEW	109
END OF THE LINE?	111

PREFACE

A while ago, I heard of an irregularity on an electrocardiogram revealing what was referred to as a "runner on the heart." It stuck with me, particularly as at the time I was pondering the philosophical connection between heart, mind, and soul.

This book, meanwhile, in its earliest guise was envisioned as a blend of poetry and prose, combining poems with short stories that would synchronize with each other. However, as time passed, and the poems came to be, I realised that they would be better suited on their own, and as I contemplated what they represented, individually and collectively, the title "Runners On The Soul" seemed very apt.

Compiled intermittently over an extremely challenging two-year period, the poems reflect the environments they were written in, as well as the events and changes that shaped my life during this time. They were written as naturally as possible, sprung from moments of inspiration, and committed to paper in the instances where creativity could thrive. While the bulk of these poems have been written in the moment, driven by the here and now, there are undoubtedly others that carry the weight of years gone by. Others, still, carry a more creative flavour, finding inspiration in unique ways, influenced by people, nature, the matter of existence, and the search for meaning and purpose.

Naturally, I am reticent to go into specific detail about the inspiration behind these poems, but I hope that preserving an air of mystery to them allows you, the reader, to find whatever you may as you go on a little journey with them, whether that be enjoyment, contemplation, or something else altogether.

WHAT'S IT ALL ABOUT?

I can't really say I understand
The praise and plaudits,
Though I'm certain many are barbed,
Though you wouldn't be surprised,
Given all the possibilities.

I nip back, looking for inspiration,
And found it.

A possibility had hovered earlier,
Though a struggle emerged,
A struggle of voice, of truth,
Of authenticity.

So many passages I wish were mine,
So influential I wish they could be,
Properly,
Without struggling with the quarries.

And again, confused by the warmth of others,
In contrast to the cold fears of future failure.

What's it all about?

Good questions are many,
Answers are few and far between,
And not always pleasant.
"Better to know an ugly truth,
Than a pretty lie."

Inspiration can be everywhere,
Which makes it even worse, sometimes.
Constantly chasing "it."
Trying to bleed wherever possible,
And every last drop, so be damned!

And still, is it good enough?
And again, what's it all about?

There are a million meanings in every line,
Most of them forgotten.
Oh, the irony...
But it's the subtlety in every line,
And what it means to every new eye
Who sees it, and sees something new,
Only to ask again:
"What's it all about?"

All too easy to look the wrong way,
And suffer the consequences,
Though art tends to be dramatic.
And so, the question is asked,
And pondered:

"Be engulfed,
Or devour it?"
Don't be surprised if the smallest,
The mere faintest,
Of chuckles escapes your throat.

More questions, more analysis,
Caught between intrigue and irritation.
So, tell me,
What's it all about?

SOMEWHERE IN THE DEPTHS

I refuse to take refuge
In what I do not know,
For ignorance is contempt for existence
And makes a vulgar show.

Words spoken can never be recovered,
The wounds from which take time to heal,
Treading lightly on bridges that can never be repaired.

Somewhere in the depths,
Stirs a trauma,
Hemorrhaging,
But it refuses to flow,
Like an ocean that forgot the damage it did
To the rock face,
And came back for more.

DREAMS

Low-key grassy knoll,
A chair, legs wedged into its Earth,
Like elsewhere.
A feline terror.
Feign death,
But eyes slightly open, hoping to escape.
Constantly glancing back,
Ready to strike, but it never pounces.
It's not like this anymore.

A jungle, not pronounced as a man would later,
Gathered beings, for what reason not clear,
And one who is loud continues to be so,
Until a simple strike leaves him no more.

The quiet water behind us,
The surroundings seem to possess a lost history.
They leave shadows upon one's soul
As we wander through them,
And one wonders if we are witnessing the actions post-sunset.
Cold & callous, why do the shadows persist?

It's over soon, but remembered, still.

There's someone there.
Please, no.
I run to escape, and instead run to face them.
It is brief.
And they're gone.

A new garden,
I see you over the fence.
What does this mean?
You say there is nothing, and there never was.
But why were you there?
New questions arise with every passing year.

A different week,
And a moment, unprecedented.
Brutal.
This could have happened.
But no answer to the knocking.
Partially revealed in four years' time.

Somebody was watching,
They were amused.
Not a care was given,
None whatsoever.
And over.

Up there, where they all gathered.
In there, where it was envisioned.
A golden experience,

With a dose of mania.
And, a family?
Those here, and those no longer,
Come to celebrate.
This happened somewhere.
I know it.

Devil's drop, we would call it.
Here, a road to a pleasant escape.
But there is no escape today.
"Do it," he orders, and his minions acquiesce.
I plead, to no avail.
I rise, and fall.
A brotherhood is broken.

I see you.
I run to you.
Everything I could possibly say, isn't said, but it is felt.
You demand, "Never again."
And it is my turn to acquiesce.
Fool.

The howls of violence reign,
And cowardice is inevitable.
She tries to intervene,
And the dreaded occurs.
The cries are enough to wake the night.

MONKEY TALES

Cautionary tales of
Motherless brides and
Pre-existing wives and
Pill-popping sides and
Overseas lies and
Blessings to the eyes
Of fools.

Decades-old notes of
Rabble rousers over the border
On a day of peace and
Sweet release!
How so?

Futuristic machinations,
Tainted fruits and
Art's creations,
And ever so
Nearer
To the end.

One monkey sipping tea,
The other reading poetry
Of a kind,
Darwinian,
Residing on a revolutionary desk,
Not knowing the many
Perplexing symbolic meanings
Placed on its shoulders
By men who thought they
Knew it all,
But what they truly knew
Only led the world astray.

Famous faces
In branded places,
Attempting to toe the line,
Invisibly,
As though one of us.

Us?

Who are we?

Butchered meats
In empty sheets,
Seeking utopian dreams
Sold at the expense
Of souls,
No refunds,
No returns.

New daughters, new sons,
And butchered bodies under
Blazing suns,
All happening concurrently,
As though every smile
Costs a frown,
Every laugh costs a tear,
And every ounce of joy
Costs a new ounce of
Hate.

NOT A CHANCE WAS STOOD

The bridges that I burnt
Were built on heaps
Of sand, and the flames
Turned the deserts into
Hell's Garden, and so
The fall of man was complete;
From the Gardens of Eden
To the ruins of Gomorrah.

The words never said
Were as loud as the dreams
That never came true.
The burden of lost hope
Is the embodiment
Of cruelty.

Not a chance was stood.

MORNING, MR. MAGPIE

There on the green by the hills,
Just prior to seeing
One of those,
Before a message is received
In a place where
Modest memories were made,
Seemingly only recent but
Further and further away,
And though you were there
At the opening,
You were gone by the close.

BOOKSHELF MUSINGS

Stories of lust from under
The Rising Sun,
Enough to make a man's
Heart swell, and
Enough to make him run.
Letters from a Stoic
In the midst of Roman rule,
Lecturing on grace and
Morality, an irony,
So cruel.
Wisdom is an affliction,
In the hands of men
Of ego,
Blessed with the gift of words
In a world with no tomorrow.
Fiction is an addiction,
In the world spoken of before,
Crippling the minds of
Millions, a world so
Spiritually poor.

EIGHT STEP

Hereditary aspirations underlie
Generational horrors,
Typical of northmen

Malignant obstacles represent
Reality's irrational sufferings

Rough and weary,
Limping impishly nevertheless,
Signalling oncoming nuances

Jokingly outrageous heresy
Now signposts ontological numbness

Carefree orchestras underpin
Lost symphonies,
Often nocturnal

Relatively overlooked brutality
Initiates neurotic sensations,
Often neglected

Love engulfs ego

Henceforth, I call Kings
Slaves

THE INITIAL CODE

Dignity issues are unavoidable,
Poverty is a way of life,
Failure is inevitable.

Lying is the devil's favourite a capella,
Motherhood is a sacred but dying art,
Fantasy is the worst form of procrastination.

Jovial tendencies are welcome to a degree,
Deprecation of the self is all too easy,
Mindless rage is rooted in blood.

Solitude is precious yet cruel,
Evolution is a teasing mystery,
Home is a destination.

Death is conceptualized by fear,
Pride is a lost art,
Faith is forgotten altogether.

Love is dying with a smile,
Madness is laughing with a tear,
Family is a painting kept in the loft.

Jokers are magnetic killers,
Dropping without control is an alternate journey,
Morning sun is an opening gambit.

Secluded souls are lost without rescue,
Excluded fools are lost without hope,
Hope is the light that never goes out.

Damaged goods are useful within reason,
People forget that they were amused,
Forgotten times are tragedies unwritten.

Lost moments occur elsewhere,
Multiversal mysteries floating in the air,
Frankly speaking, we know absolutely nothing.

Jingoistic types often mean well,
Distorted ideals are a sin of collectives,
Much maligned dreams never seem to pass.

Sanctimonious beings are many,
Erroneous acts are without recovery,
Hegemonic power is lost to others.

Dread is a lingering odour,
Power is a lustful whore,
Forgiveness is forever in short supply, and sometimes rightly so.

Lethargy is an enemy of triumph,
Mind games are a waste of chess,
Fruitful endeavours are often abandoned.

Judgement is never too far,
Delicate insinuations only distort your pathway,
Meandering through life causes only disappointment.

Seduction is a hellish attempt at divinity,
Enveloping actions lead one astray,
Hedonism is humanity's way of abandoning all hope.

Deities will be surprised upon their return,
Parental misgivings that kids never learn,
Followers laugh when they hit the abyss.

Loaded guns may or may not set you free,
Malignant forces by one and by three,
Fright is awakening when you forgot you were asleep.

Jealousy is pitiful when contrasted with envy,
Demands are made by those on hollow ground,
Mistakes are made for no reason whatsoever.

Space is there yet so far away,
Enduring nostalgia is a prison itself,
Holistic methods are never truly achieved.

Destruction is a pin drop in a world of noise,
Privacy is REDACTED,
Fondness comes in the simplest ways.

Learning is endless, but often without result,
Misery is a business, taken from above,
Flickering lights mean more than you realise.

Jesters were the Kings all along,
Diatribes without purpose are a sign of madness,
Memberships are exclusive and worthless.

School days never leave you, for better and for worse,
Endings are beginnings, until no beginnings remain,
Hotel Life is a semi-permanent stay.

Disease is modern life; incurable,
Passion is meaningless without direction,
Falsehoods create a sorry state of affairs.

Lovers aren't friends; they're so much more,
Mothers who cry break the hearts of angels,
Fathers who fail are burdened completely.

Juggernaut brothers can never be understood,
Destitute areas are rotting as we speak,
Maybe, you don't really wanna know.

Souls drift with each passing sin,
Escalations lead to the road to nowhere,
Heavy is the heart that cares too much.

THE SIBLING GAME

Do you ever stop and wonder?
And yes, I already know the answer.
No, that won't stop me from asking.
I come back to it so often,
Every time wondering, "what if?"
Life was never meant to bring us together,
Lost is any hope of defying the odds.
Everywhere, I'm reminded.

Lest I forget, my foolish errors,
Of course, the faults were mine,
Understandable, is your distaste.
I, these days, reside in the shadows,
Sibling unwanted, and unspoken of.
Everywhere, I'm reminded.

Just one joke would make me choke,
And yet, I laugh, all the same.
Crucifixion of the hopes and dreams
Kicked the bucket on the sibling game.

LIFE'S TRUTHS AND CRIMES

Doves made from heels,
And the pain you feel is insolent in the face of truth,
Of life's truths and crimes,
And all its little moments
That you can never enjoy.

Drifting from a distance
Wondering, pondering,
Pointlessly so.

Each key another hammer to the heart,
To the soul.

Each howl another tear on the canvas of the mind,
Each word a call to arms in the heart of man,
In the soul of woman,
In the essence of species,
And the destiny of existence.

RIVERS, LIKE POETIC SPEECHES

Rivers, like poetic speeches,
Cascade like blissful divinity,
A showcase of water's
Representation of nature,
In its contrast to all around it.

The flow is a show of strength,
But its journey is uncertain,
For it knows not if it will
Achieve the brilliance of
Reconciliation with the seas,
Or whether it will meander
Into the streams,
Completing at a point unseen,
And uncared for.

The journey is a dream
Without the pettiness of articulation,

The need for absolute definition
In a world where truth is unspoken,
For the people cannot comprehend
Its power, nor its reality.

The water knows not the futility
Of man, or dreams,
But somewhere on the journey,
For the briefest moment,
It will share with men
The great unknown, and
The great unanswered,
Until the answer finally comes.

THE PARK

Earth everywhere,
And its air envelopes you in its chill,
Cruel yet appreciated.

No one dare look, repugnant it must be.

Why do they slip when they walk on by?
Or, how do they avoid it?

Heartbreak, a life like this.

Passing by, not a shred of knowledge,
Or understanding.
Why would they?

That's all for now.

SEPTEMBER 18TH

Tranquil conditions, tinted with harsh realities,
As generations come together,
Sharing soul & mind, a bond of blood.

Memories & expressions are laid on the table,
Tales of hardship, pearls of wisdom,
In a place where gratitude is shown & appreciated.

For every smile, tears of woe,
For every mouth fed, a body below,
For every spoon, a knife in tow.

Spots & dots fall through the trees,
Dripping to the Earth, evading the breeze,
And as each drop hits the ground below,
A bloodline bond begins to show.

HORROR, STRIFE, MANIA, ANXIETY

Deep, deep down the rabbit hole,
Longer than we could imagine,
Beyond the point of no return.
Rage, fury, hate & woe,
And a cruel little cup of bitterness.
Demented delusion from head to toe,
And a mask of demonic contortion.
Bridges burn & bridges fall,
Just as they always have.
Roads are closed and pathways soiled,
By the actions of sociopaths.
Shiver, tremble, stutter, scream,
The makings of a darkened dream.
Run, hide, crouch, crawl,
And pray to find heaven's hall.

"WALL"

I sat, perched, and yet exposed,
In a place I should never have been,
But you told me,
"I can't wait,"
And you told me all your dreams,
And what you wanted to do,
And I nearly drowned in your
Fantasies, until I realised
I was able to swim away
From the beasts lying in wait
On the ocean floor,
And though your accented desires
Could have torn my soul apart,
We simply parted,
Embittered and confused,
Left without satisfaction,
And again, strangers we became.

AT LEAST YOUR SONG IS PLAYING

They're not talking to you,
No one is,
Pull those claws down,
Put them away.
Still hitting walls?
It's your fault you can't see,
They think you're fine,
"But they don't know me,"
And nobody wants to.
Choke like everybody does,
But for you there is no reward,
No happy ending,
Barely an outcome at all.
Just be grateful for breathing,
At least your song is playing,
Again.

TOUCHED BY FLAMES

Find what you wish you could through all the noise,
Make all the participants in the game your toys,
Only to realise that the more you treat life as a game,
You only end up playing yourself.

Pull and pull back on yourself,
Not sure whether to go, or even where.
How can you unwrap yourself from the chains
Of others when you continue to chain yourself?

These journeys will only darken you,
Like they do over, and over again.
Through all the battered alleyways and scattered debris,
You're still exactly where you were.

The aching in one shares the sound of the aching of another.
The genius of one can match the genius of five.
A single song can evoke the memories of a lifetime.

Such a crack in the wall, until beauty reveals itself.

Why do they always come back to you?
It could apply to anybody, any of the others,
But still you persist,
Without even knowing it.

Amazing how the words of one can speak for millions.

KHARMIC CONSEQUENCES

An old book from some years ago
Hosted notes and scribbles,
Desperately gathered
In the hope of success.
Now, it is bare,
The old notes either discarded,
Or saved elsewhere.

In the back lies an address
I wasn't expecting to see.
Much like looking back
On the book's early days,
I see the address
And wonder,
"Was it real?"
Or,
"Was it really so long ago?"

After a brief flurry,
I've lost sight of why,
Much like then.
There is no control,
No composure,
Only confusion,
Regret,
Pain.

This requires grit,
In times of crises.
Inevitable questions arise
In such times,
And certain answers have
Grave consequences.

Other questions are presented
Of a more philosophical nature,
Asking,
"What had occurred before all this?"
If such a thing exists.
Is karma present?
If so, its cruelty is truly apparent.

But then, what of the
Earliest days?
Was karma in play at
The very beginning?
Was sixteen days late pushing it
Somewhat?

Distractions emerge,
And maybe for the best,
However briefly they may linger.
A reorganisation produced basic results,
The trimming continues,
However slowly,
However methodically.

VALENTINE & POE

Valentine quoted Poe
When war descended
On the people.

The children suffered
When tolerance became
An unfortunate convenience.

Blood was spilt
When invisible demons
Uttered heinous myths.

A villain's death
Was twisted for
Flexible creative endeavour.

Darkness reigned supreme
Over light when
Valentine quoted Poe.

GOLDEN HEEL

You were like nothing I had
Experienced,
And so quickly you
Embedded yourself in my mind,
Still occupying a place.
It amused you, later on,
Hence your revelation.
Your sweetness contrasted
With your venomous vibe,
Your delicacy with your bite.
You felt fragile,
But you could not be broken,
Like a china doll that
Could never shatter,
And you knew all along,
Though it did not matter.

THURSDAY MORNING JOURNEY

Stood in the cold, what do I feel?
Dreaming of you, when will it heal?
You, in the sky, what say you?
You, up there, with the purest blue.

Completely dry, washed all over,
Blanketed by guilt, dampened by doubt.
I need your company, as usual,
Subtle, yet undeniable, an aid.

A realisation, let it drop,
One-step, two-step, let it drop.
But I might be wrong, but let us see.

Morning headlines, jagged as usual,
Swallowed by commercialism, an irony.
One arrives, but the wait goes on,
As is often the case.

A "new" one plays, better than I realised,
Ideologically synchronized.

The steps are silent, to me at least,
An arrival, but hardly a feast.
No sign of you this morning,
Just the dregs and the occasional yawning.

Bring it down to rubble and waste,
And in its place grow fields of green,
Imagine a little scene so serene,
Amidst this dump of a town with such poor taste.

The sun can burn brightest through layers of glass,
Upon layers of people with no such class.
An imaginary jazz bar beckons,
As I leave this place of sloppy seconds.

Fear remains, and fear rules,
In the minds of those who left it to rot.
Fear will thrive, and fear will reign,
In the minds of those who know nothing else.

Slightly quicker, yet at the same pace,
In the reflection, a shadowed face.
Questions asked, and questions pondered,
Are answers even possible?

Follow the voices, the worms, the fishes,
And the beautiful haunting.

We won't get the chance, though we dream,
We'll all belong to them,
Regardless of the final choice we make.
That'll be some journey.

You're late.

That's why I avoid it.
I can't do it anymore.
Funny what remains, even at this tender stage,
As others declare a state of engage.

A few months have passed,
I wonder if they've been spun since.
Looks like there's a decision to be made,
What do you reckon?

A DEADPAN NOTE

I wrote a note in my head
But never made it to bed,
Or at least, that was the plan.
I met some people in dreams
That came apart at the seams,
Same as always, a flash in the pan.
I found some hope with a rope,
I guess I felt I could cope,
Or is this where all this began?
I tasted bliss under the light,
About four hours before midnight,
And she wafted those fingers like a fan.
I took some money from the poor,
Working for the rich is such a chore,
Please sir, put my pennies in the can.
I broke hearts, I was told,
Losing love turned my own cold,
And before you lies the shell of a forgotten man.

THE KING

Most precious little being,
Gifted to us by happenstance and opportunity.
Born Scouse, Adopted Manc,
This world was never enough, nor could it ever be.

I realise, as time passes, how fortunate my life was
To be blessed by such an interruption.
Through all the trials and tribulations,
Every scar was worth it, and every scar suffered was nothing
Compared to the one left behind, the one that will never heal.

Love is the finest thing.
I often say, "Wanna know it means to be human? Fall in love!"
Ironic choice of words in these circumstances,
Wouldn't you say?
This is what you inspired: love!

Only now do I find the words I couldn't truly on that final day,
But I hope my service was enough when the time came,
And as I said that fateful day, "I will see you again!"

EVERY ONCE IN A WHILE…

Contradictory themes paint a picture,
Complete with colours never seen,
And thus, not understood.

Falsehoods flourish under good intentions,
Offered by those who know less,
Yet know so much more.

Fractured beliefs meet broken dreams,
Broken mirrors reflect shattered souls,
As shattered minds stumble and fall.

Even a clown can take centre stage,
Every once in a while…

LOST MOMENTS?

Imagine mourning what never was,
And what was never meant to be,
And, if honesty may flourish,
What was never even desired.
And yet, as years do pass,
A light is shone on possibilities
That drift deftly into the shadows,
Further and further away,
Never to be realised,
Nor even understood.

THREE LINE WHIP

Words previously written
Have been discarded
With violent vigour.

A conglomerate surname
Times by two
Equals the truth.

Hearts and Souls
Have been fractured,
But not broken.

Encouragement was given
To the dreamer
Who cannot launch.

A man who
Once spoke loudest,
Now says nothing.

A BRANCH

And to think,
You thought you were in control.
In this story of war and peace,
How could such an arrogance have thrived?

Like it always does, I suppose.

You fear their judgements,
But they have tread this journey.
Their story is yours.
You are a branch.

THE LOST WOMAN

A mother cradles the baby
She never knew,
Canned in at the temporary terminal,
Addled beyond repair,
Only as she is, and
Only as you can be
In such circumstances
As these,
Casting fungi into the lungs
Of others,
The spread of mild plague
Both biological and spiritual,
Coughing both guts and dreams into
The sewers,
Where they face their destiny,
Fed on by the vermin of
The underground,
The final destination of the deceased
In misery.

TRANQUIL IS THE STREAM

Tranquil is the stream,
But still a man seeks fish,
Not realising that,
Though the fish are to be cherished,
They are nothing in comparison to the water,
Just as humans are nothing compared to the air.

Subtle is the way of nature,
Of speaking to the soul,
Bypassing our basic instincts,
Able to touch what still we fail to grasp.

A thousand years I could stand,
Watching, listening,
As the tranquil stream lives a life beyond my own,
And beyond that of any being on Earth.

FAREWELL TO THE POSSESSIONS

Farewell to the possessions,
Casualties of a battle of the spirit.
How I dreamed of decoration,
Only to lose sight of the majesty
Of words.
How I dreamed of decoration,
Only to remember an audience
Of one.

The words of Swan '91 ring true,
To a certain degree and
From a certain point of view.
Put into the world what
You have loved,
What can no longer be
Taken with you,
And allow it to bring
Joy to the lives of others.

TODAY IT WAS CLEAR

Glancing over old notes,
Thinking how today I realised,
"It wasn't meant to be like this."
I already knew that,
But today it was clear,
As though a mist had lifted
From the Island,
Giving sight to the blind,
As though what they had seen before
Had been a charade.

At the same time,
I think of how I'm trying.
Trying to give up
On what cannot be,
And wondering whether stubbornness
Is an admirable trait,
Or merely an unbreakable wall,
Built on the whims and wishes
Of a fool.

Enthusiasm breeds hope,
Like pouring fuel on the fire
Of dreams,
Setting visions alight,
Edging the border of hallucination.

Are the idiots easily led,
Or is the "leader" the fool
For viewing them as such,
And as a result,
Failing before he has even begun?

02:03

We're here, again,
In the dead of night.

The irony will never be lost on me,
To suffer through the hideous nature of ideation,
Only to fear the very threat of death
When he seemingly comes knocking.
Notice the lack of Death's presence,
But simply the possibility of his arrival is
Enough to make a mockery of other crippling intrusions.

We've been here before,
Not always in the night.

Like the strains of a child pulling the string
That unleashes a little wonder,
But feeling like the battering waves those beasts endure,
Reminding oneself of the contrast
Between reality and illusion,
Between conquest and fear,
Between life and "death."

We'll be here, again,
Anytime, anywhere.

Every trip is a lesson,
Every journey a lecture,
Every conclusion a source of feedback.
To come through the other side exposes reality,
To embrace that reality is a show of strength.
This is how things are now,
These are the cards life has dealt us.

TT-MH

Clutching at strings for levers
To pull back the curtains
Hiding the truths,
Clutching at straws for a taste
Of that that is so sweet,
All while finding fear at
Walking the line walked
A thousand times before.

Hearing the sounds that provoke
The chains of nostalgia,
Walking blindly into traps
Laid by art of an
Unappreciated quality,
Music the masses would
Fail to understand,
The sweet hauntings of
A man who abandoned
Money for acclaim,
Who was capable of
Joyful brilliance, but instead chose

To speak to souls willing to hear
Beyond the norm,
And were taken as a result.

When art fails to birth,
We look to the art of others
To explain our souls,
But instead, present false exhibitions,
The stories of others,
Not ourselves,
And so, we too often bury
Our own art in favour
Of silence,
And thus rob the world
Of a museum unlike any other,
One of life and humanity,
Of our purpose and pretention,
Of our questions and our answers.

THE FALLING CURTAIN

It never used to matter,
Until one night the curtains
Threatened to fall,
And in my slumber, I found
Myself hounded by a horror,
Modest yet unspeakable.
It happened over and over,
Lured into sleep with such ease,
Before so quickly returning, like
A man fleeing what he
Cannot understand.
In time, I gave up,
Acquiescing to this unpleasant
Mystery, limited in choice
By necessity, and now
I don't sleep that way anymore.

NIGHTHAWK

Laid down under the crucifying weight of existence,
And an excruciating lack of real knowledge.

Crippled by the indignation of longing and
Reaching for the untouchable.

Lost in a misty abyss of conscious sleepwalking
And blind-alley exploration.

Consumed by the sounds of magic,
Long lost & irreplaceable.
Blanketed in a false web of discovery,
Right back to where you began.

Toes tipping to something you don't belong to,
And never could, for all your efforts.

Distracted by voices indefinable,
Whose tones may once have haunted,
But now seem so welcoming.

Allured by a time so fraught,
Which once seemed so horrifying,
And in reality,
Was and is,
But still seems so much better than what's to come.

Lost in the sugar-coated escapism of what has gone,
Dreading the hedonistic nihilism that awaits us all.

SEPTEMBER, 15TH

Train tracks glow in the midday light,
In contrast to the internal dark.
Addled thoughts are rampant elsewhere,
And here, not entirely stable.

Somewhere, a body distraught craves answers,
And how they are achieved remains the question,
But the end is nowhere near in sight.

Nearer, an opportunity could present itself,
But even fools must know when not to cross a broken bridge.

On the other side of town, lies the one,
But the one never was, and so that must be laid to rest.

Even further away, tea is made,
And the beverage itself,
Storming inside its porcelain prison,
Represents more than it can possibly imagine.

If happiness is a warm gun, then loneliness is a setting sun.

WORDS WITH A LADY OF GOD

A film awaits, and so travel is made,
A driver with little sense makes an error,
But he corrects himself,
And we continue.

A conversation is had at the back of a bus,
Often the scene of such instances.
Reflections are exchanged, failures noted, tragedies identified.
Culture & Community are mourned,
Nihilism & Decadence are loathed.

Stories, watered down, are shared,
And a mutual desire for good is expressed.
She makes reference to the Kingdom of God,
But I miss it, and we continue.
As we reach our destination, she reveals herself.
The Kingdom is highlighted once more,
And I realise what is in front of me.

I note my recent pondering on deity,
And whether it currently finds itself travelling the Universe,
Having forgotten about us for the time being,
And whether upon its return to Earth,
It shall realise the fall of humanity in its absence.

Humoured, but cheered also,
Hands are shaken,
And goodbyes are said.

And little did I know, the film wasn't there at all.

ATONEMENT & FAITH

I know it should end but
It will not leave me alone,
Just when you think there is
Nothing left to atone,
You see a face in the mirror that
You struggle to recognise,
In the midst of a web of lies
That are merely distorted truths
Lost in a wave of confusion and
Abandonment of faith that was
Never there to begin with.

TAKE, SEEK, FIND

Take me at my weakest,
Take me when it's true.
Fool me at my strongest,
So I know it's you.
Turn me at my truest,
When I'm truly blind.
Seek me at my lowest,
And see just what you find.
Truly find a truth,
To truly know a lie.

HAS IT BEGUN?

Am I fading?
Has it begun?
Has the stitching come undone?

As we wonder through forests,
Long cut down,
Feet crunching twigs that have longed turned to dust,
Seeing life where it once lived,
An echo in time that must not be forgotten.
We owe it to them.

But am I losing?
Am I snoozing?
Stumbling through a haze that's bruising.

How do I decide, when all is distorted?
When what made sense is fading,
Passing into an ether,
Of which I know no definition,
Only silence, all of a sudden.
Has it begun?

POISONOUS REFLECTIONS

Are dreams destroyed in seconds,
Or notions?
Maybe more through revelations,
Or the acknowledgement of
Poisonous reflections.

For the words laid down
On paper,
And the thoughts never expressed,
I can only apologise,
And paint a picture of
An unfortunate reality,
Corrupted by loss and lust,
Held together by chemistry,
And desperation,
Uttering words glued together
By me,
But fermented elsewhere.

DESTITUTE DREAMS

It is like destitution in a way,
Feeding on you in the moments
You try so desperately,
Only to tear away at the roots,
Pounding away in frustration,
Staring into nowhere.

Picture a blank canvas,
But envisage it coated in glory,
In art that bypasses the need
For verbal articulation,
Representing more than mere
Dialogue definition can provide.
And now, look back at the
Canvas, still blank, still void
Of the art as imagined,
For its creation is a dream,
And though dreams may birth
New realities, reality is
A limited dream.

REFLECTING ON A WORK

He just had a flick through,
Thousands of words,
Some partially true.

Never had been much of a fan,
But inspiration came,
He was a different man.

So many ideas requiring execution,
Some big, some small, a mind's persecution.

Standalones and prequel tones,
Big things have small beginnings,
Others just stand in stone.

Dark dream inspiration,
For some that is, but for others,
Unfinished irritation.

Tales of a bygone age,
Others of a more recent flavour,
Splattered across every page.

Notice the subtleties of those who inspired,
From doctors & lords
Whose impact was admired.

Fractured minds and broken souls,
Haunting letters and tainted homes,
Burning schools and bleeding holes.

Deep space disaster for worn out friends,
Tragic histories and tales anew,
The seeds for stories that may never end.

Held in your hand is the effort of a man,
After failures galore,
Just to show that he can.

NOT EVEN HERE

Not even here,
With these broken and decayed,
Can a man find solitude and friendship.
Not even here,
Among the dregs, the aimless,
Can a man find his people.

Isolation amongst the normals,
That's one thing.
Isolation amongst the rest,
That's another thing altogether.

The people.
Those idealistic people.
They simply don't exist.
They never did.
They never will.

SCARS FROM THE CROWN

These scars from the crown of thorns
You cannot see, wrapped around with
Malice and malpractice,
Symbolical of internal warfare,
The overflow of acidic waste
Rising from the ugliest depths
To make its presence known
And felt, exposing itself
And its victim for all to see,
As the crowds who taunted
The prophet fail to make
An effort, and the work of
Evil is in petty vain,
A show of tortured excess
For the benefit of no one,
Except to show the man in the mirror
What a mess he has truly become.

MISGUIDED CALLINGS

Icebergs and wallflowers
Make for a unique blend of
Inspiration and motivation
Beside a white night light,
An insomniac's kryptonite.

Compounds and nightclubs
Are the realms of
Misguided callings,
Ambulance sirens providing
A fitting wake-up call
In differing circumstances.

Sandy dunes of the poor
And the oil rich
Provide contrasting romantic awakenings,
All the more sobering
When naive pinings
Produce Arabian laughs
And golden mania.

MONDAY, 5TH

Caught me off guard, typical.

Like a bolt most desired, seemingly anticipated,
But in truth never prepared for.

Only brief,
Your moves along the floor displaying character,
And so, we engage.
Only good vibes, a kind of magnetism about you.
At ease.

It's over, rather quickly.
Your gaze modestly burns itself into my mind, a sweetness.

I'm reminded again how difficult this is,
And of my own fragility.

See you around, maybe.

DON'T GIVE UP

Delirium, or delusion.
This is fear to me, and this is somewhere I don't want to be.
This is the reality in the face of the jokes of insanity,
Where we laugh with our crude little fantasies
About losing our minds,
When the truth is so much worse.

This is the hole you never wanted to fall into,
Because you never knew it existed.
This is the hole you wish the dirt would follow you into,
When in the cruellest of moments, you fear there is no return.

Leave your gimmicks at the door,
Spiritually, you're hideously poor.
Succumb to fantasies at your own peril,
If you truly wish to know what it means to be feral.
You pluck the blisters out on your way back,
You're on a new journey, on a beaten track.

Failure is inevitable, but pain is temporary.
Don't give up.

R2

As it turns out, differences were substantial, but nevermind.

Funny how these things occur,
Such is the nature of happenstance.

Good vibes aplenty, and a chuckle, too,
And now the sound of home beckons to you.

Thanks for the direction, however unintentional.

A STORY ENDS AND A STORY BEGINS

A baby is born, but a mother is lost,
As roads become rivers in the downpour.
Journeys undertaken and purchases made,
But are the lives that we live
Worth the prices we paid?

News is broken, but reaction is muted,
As faraway dreams threaten to make a scene.
Violence rules but silence reigns;
Is this why instead of building bridges,
We choose to play these games?

Wounds are left, scars will show,
It couldn't be any other way.
As one story ends, another has begun,
But can we truly say
That the best is yet to come?

COLD REVELATONS

Selective pinings for voids
That cannot be filled,
An errant game built
On foundations of
Well-intentioned hopes
And dreams,
But washed away by
Tsunamis triggered by
Cold revelations.

IDEATION vs. FEAR

Chronic, as it was, still can be.
Ironic, as you were, given the contrast.
Inspired by discontent, dissatisfaction,
Loathing, hopelessness, guilt.
Prevented only by cowardice, and a sense of loyalty.

When other histrionic sensations occur,
The ideation cowers into the corner,
Feeble & exposed.

Its malice is clear to see, as a desire for life,
Or at least a more ideal end,
Comes to the surface.

For every cut, and every wound,
There is an attack on the senses.
For every drop of blood,
There is a teardrop.

For every plea for it to end,
There is a cry for survival.

And it never ends,
This battle of fatality.
All in the mind and soul of a man
So insignificant,
So meagre,
So worthless.

A death would mean so, so little,
But still life persists.

THE SPARK OF LIFE

This is why I sit here waiting,
Procrastinating, anticipating,
Seeking a spark that is seemingly
Deserting,
And fittingly so,
When the balance of
Patience and eagerness is so
Blitheringly impossible to achieve.
Seek or wait?
Wait or seek?
And how to be ready when
It strikes you when you are
Neither seeking nor waiting...

A CREATIVE MAN'S BURDEN

So easy it is for a man to pause,
And to take stock of his situation,
And of his attempts.
In doing so, he so quickly feels fraudulent.

He wears a mask almost permanently,
But can't bear the thought of one representing fallacy,
Even though that's exactly what every mask represents.

He listens, and is inspired.
He reads, and is motivated.
He watches, and dreams.
He aspires, and desires.

And still, he feels fraudulent.

He wishes to be himself,
But that isn't wanted by anybody.

He wishes to leave a legacy,
But all the legends have come and gone.
He wishes to leave a mark,
But simply leaves them on himself.
He becomes the canvas,
And realises that regardless of his insecurities,
He must press on.

He is the art,
His mind is the machine,
And his fingers are the instruments.

A TINY TRAGEDY

Merely a splatter, whipper snapper,
That took its life, as a factual matter,
To us, a mere drop,
To it, a full stop.

Lost, like a child in a marketplace,
With a being, so large, couldn't see its face.

Spawned away, a journey begun,
But ended so soon, not a chance to run.

Raindrops fell, and teardrops, too,
For this was the tragedy
Of me and you.

PAUSING AGAIN

Pausing again,
To much irritation,
Just to spill some more
Useless thoughts and feelings
Of no value to anyone,
But overflowing an open-topped flask
Like first-time tourists falling
From an open-top bus in the
Midst of an unnecessary frenzy,
Crumbling at the feet of
Unamused passersby,
Who pass on by with
Frowns, hounds, and gowns,
Bleeding grey emotions into a
World increasingly devoid of
Real colour.

Pausing again,
To a lack of amusement,
Just to unload a barrage
Of ideas and musings,

Barricaded by frustration
And chained by a lack of
Invitation to be freed with
A sense of order and stability,
Instead meandering blindly into
Oncoming traffic, and crushed by
Drivers with little concern,
While fresh onlookers shrug and
Carry on, keeping on keeping on,
But with only just enough energy
To exist, not to live,
To lay but not to love,
To speak but to say nothing.

Pausing again,
To little acknowledgement,
Just to monologue a memory
Combined with a revelation
So worthless that not even
Dust could be disturbed,
While tired eyes grow heavier,
And weary ears close shut,
Dialogue remains on its one-way
Trajectory, down a pathway
Long abandoned and forgotten,
But followed down by the only
One who ever could,
For it is theirs and theirs alone,
And though this road is a lonely
And pathetic one, it still exists,
And thus, until it can be tread no more,

It shall still play host to the
Echoes of thoughts and feelings,
Ideas and musings,
And many, many a monologue.

BOUNCING OFF THE WALLS

Stains on my shoes
From singing the Blues,
Pouring out barely diluted
Diatribes over brews,
Feet on the table
With everything to lose,
Yet there is nothing left.

"Happy" faces come easy,
Exposing that human pining
For joy amidst the echoes
Of misery,
The howls of beasts bouncing
Off the walls,
Forming the soundtrack of
What seems inevitable,
And always has, and yet,
Nothing is for sure.

Knocking on stone floors,
Hoping for reverberations
That reveal new opportunities,
New discoveries,
New reasons to keep going,
To fill another page,
To amuse the masses,
To fill the void of purpose.

Tears are held back and
Choked on,
Until eyes weep like
Sores expelling fluids,
Clean-up on Aisle 5,
Just a reminder to stay alive.

AIR

Take me in the arms
That only you possess,
Bless me with the love
That wipes away the distress.
Remind me of the truth
That I so often forget,
Gift me with the finest scenery
Before the autumn sunset.
Cushion me from sounds
That crucify the soul,
Protect me with the shields
That ensure I remain whole.
Allow these tears to fall
Upon your hallowed ground,
And may they give the gift of growth
So it all comes back around.

HE'S LONG FORGOTTEN

Two monkeys, a dog, and a trooper,
All stare into a light,
While a man stares at a door.
He's scraping at the bottom of a well,
But struggling to find any more.

A villain, a brush, and a bundle of books,
Stand collectively as one,
Near scents and smells,
Swigs and picks,
And a bottle of whiskey, not rum.

Altogether, a world within a world,
Unseen and untouched,
By the rest, outside.

He's long forgotten.

SAME OLD

Same old words, same old topics,
Try a new gimmick, perhaps?

Same old cliches, same old road,
All while you watch it collapse.

Same old diversions, same old dreams,
Stuck on 4th and 1.

Same old waste, same old tropes,
This isn't about anyone else.

A STORY OF MEN

A man gave love,
And all who received give thanks,
But his weakness showed,
And those he failed suffered the most.
A man loved, but fell.

A man desired love,
And found it too late,
But better late than never,
After all those merry dances.
A man loved, but falls.

A man knew only pain,
Always did, and likely always will,
A pain we cannot define,
Despite all we try.
A man loved, but will fall.

A TUB OF HUMAN WINE

A tub of human wine
From a single sinful crime,
Where the howls of
Demons and false gods
Led a man to a door,
And in his hand, he held
The key of no return
In the form of a blade.

In this tub of human wine
Of the cruellest, impure kind,
A story so nearly reached its
Conclusion,
But instead, only saw
The beginning of a new chapter,
One which would forever
Bare the scars of the words
Laid down on previous pages.

This tub of human wine,
Emptied away like a departed tide,
Taking with it a moment of horror,
And a day of torment,
But in its passing,
Survival shone through,
And so, the story continued,
And as the wine sank
Away to the shore,
A room became no more.

DISORDERLY

Waterfalls don't end, or so it seems,
Thunderstorms are eternal, only in dreams.

It's what come after that matters,
Paradoxical symptoms and a Cheshire grin,
Singing and shouting and dreaming of sin.
Waste not, want not, no reply,
Write some words, say goodbye.

I'm losing the spirit, but I've got the feeling...

AND YET…

Back in that place that has
Sprung new vigour,
New dawns for old times,
Old experiences given new life,
But searching, hunting,
For analogies and artistic
Representation of everything,
From the mundane to the insane,
From fright to delight,
From above and for the love.

Dipping my toes into lavas
Just for a response,
To break the cycle of
Smashing my head against the wall,
Ox-style.

Asking the same question
Over and over,
Like a dying man drinking
From a puddle,

While the world walks by him,
But doesn't realise he's there.

Reading the words of a
Woman whose intensity
Burns from the pages,
Whose art reflects love
At its purest, and yet its darkest.

And still, I yearn for more.
Still hoping to wrench more
From my soul,
Despite the music having ended,
The waters drying up,
The fires falling away.

And yet...

WE?

Who knew,
That the brightest light
Exposed the things in the dark,
The things we fear to know,
The things we cannot define.

Changes have occurred,
And yet we did not know.
The feeling feeds an unarticulated fear;
How could we not have known?

We?

DARK AURAS

The future was feared then,
And rightly so.
Just as today,
And rightly so.
Skies were blanketed,
An aura shared by
Day-to-day existence,
Cold and haunting,
Breeding fear,
And nightmares.

So many a night was ruined.

Now, it barely seems real,
To look back at what was.
Time and memories betray us
With their fluidity,
Their mysticism a twisted game.

What was so short,
Felt so long.

Now what seems a lifetime,
Feels like yesterday.
What felt like a
Child's worst fears,
Have become a man's
Reality.

The soul of the seasons
Remains the same,
Just the man who walks
The scene,
Who wears an older face,
Who gazes with wearier eyes.

If only he had known.

I WALKED, AND I WALK

I walked, as I walk,
On endless wire,
Atop pathways tread by millions,
Beneath the shimmering light
Of the Gods,
In the day,
And in the night.

I walked in the early mornings,
Along roads known,
But not like this,
Changed as with all things
In the passage of time,
And from an angle
Not previously taken.
Estates and woodland ways
Succeeded concrete runways,
Leading to fields and farms,

A majesty blended with abject
Normality,
A place which found itself
Sneered at by so many,
But called to those
Willing to listen,
Like all the finest things.
It was during this time that
Eras ended,
Streaks were broken,
Warriors fell,
And landmarks were reached,
While the eternal trappings
Of false dawns caught
Victims galore,
As they have before,
And shall do so again.
An innovation brought crashing waves
To a flow where crashing waves
Had already resided,
But with new impetus.
The cattle watched in bemusement
As they always did,
And their presence was loved,
Until it was no more,
And the Void's own cruel presence
Was harsher than what had
Come before.
Still, at least the ants
Had their new home,
Their colony in the arteries

Of the off-road forests
Unbeknownst to so many
A passer-by,
As is often the case.
A climb is often representative
Of human struggle,
And this was no different,
As the morning sun
Crossed over and allowed the
Persistent moon to clock off
Until later.
At the very top,
After tapping into nature's beauty
To beat back the struggle,
A familiar old temple came into view,
Its increasing loneliness
A sad state of affairs,
And yet the nature of my
Love affair with the natural world,
In contrast to the decline of
The holy house,
Bred a contrast that becomes
Ever more apparent as the
Years pass by.

I walk, changed from the passing years,
But fuelled by desperation all the same.
Where often I am accompanied
By the sounds of generations,
Instead, a voice tells a story,
And it is perfect,

A companionship made for
Such a setting.
The climb is early,
And so, the challenge
Must be met head-on,
The suffering coming during
The easy part.
The tale of those who
Pulled strings in the shadows,
Who lived and died
By the sword,
Corrupted by hate and betrayal,
In the pursuit of
Absolute power,
Is detailed in the
Most beautiful way,
Alongside accounts of
Other worlds,
And the nature of species,
And another,
And another...
Here, though, is where roots
Can be found,
Like elsewhere relatively nearby.
I gaze to where they lived,
Trying, maybe, to confirm
What came before,
But the mind struggles to comprehend,
Despite knowing the truth.
That child-like notion of
Failing to fathom

What it cannot deem familiar
Brings frustration,
But it soon passes.
The winds push me along,
Where previously they held me back,
And I hold myself in a
State of content.
The story continues,
As it shall do so,
With the rooftops and
Distant hilltops combining
To create an art piece
Known only to me,
And when it flows,
I am the luckiest
Man in the world.

BUT…

Echoes in a cave that never fade away,
Like a howling cacophony sent to
Finish the job,
Or, at the very least,
Nudge things along.
But that can go either way…

Sliding the dial brought
Such delight, though one fears
Poisoning another's art,
A fear intensified by one's own love
For the art in question.
But it was so good…

A sense of familiarity in a
World of differences is such
A peculiar thing,
As though we find unity and harmony
In division and chaos.
But then, how typically human…

A mind that has never known mania
Can never truly appreciate peace,
For it has only known the tranquility
Of serenity, and has never journeyed
Through the inferno.
But some are so lucky...

I WALKED, IN THE EVENINGS

I walked in the evenings,
Chasing an idea that
Became a reality,
Eventually.
While the realities of one dream
Exposed themselves as false Gods,
This one was of a material nature,
And yet biological,
And, thus, absolutely essential.
As ever, a conclusive climb
Provided a fitting challenge,
But to conquer it was to conquer
The Devil himself,
For this was his drop,
Our youthful selves were told.

CONTRADICTORY ANECODTES ON A LOST "LOVE"

<u>*Truthfully Speaking*</u>
Angel eyes, smooth as silk,
Heaven to touch, the finest ilk.

So easily a man can fall to such beauty,
Blinded by awe,
Reality a distant memory.

In the midst of euphoria, foolishness sets in.
The possibility of devastating mistakes grows with each
Passing day, hour, minute, second.

Sweet, short moments we would share,
Each night our love was in the air.

But, was love ever truly there?

Maybe, in the midst of such intensity, love did blossom,
Albeit like a flower sprung up in the wrong field.
After all, that is what we were,
In the wrong place at the wrong time.
Regardless, even under the darkest of skies,
And the cruellest of nights,
I would have set the world alight
Just so we could have danced on its ashes.

In truth, her love belongs elsewhere,
And that love should blossom, if life is fair.
Fear not for me, dear angel eyes,
Our fates were sealed when we said our goodbyes.

For That...
I let go of the second one,
But not the first.
The one from that night where we walked,
Sneaking little shows of affection behind a figure of disgust.

We held, like lovers do, along a road lit by a blend of
Moonlight and artificiality,
And neither light could compare with your glow.

Nights like those are cherished,
However few and far between,
And however misguided.
You gave me more than you could ever realise,
And for that I thank you.
For that, I loved you.

You Were A Gun

Though the song's beauty masks our vulgarity,
You were a gun I held to my head.
Though I knew truly what a mistake you were,
The beast needed to be fed.
Though all along you were driven by lust,
Love's false journey was led.
Though even now the scars still linger,
Things are better left unsaid.

A WOMAN I NEVER KNEW

A woman I never knew,
But whose actions impacted
My very existence.

A woman I never knew,
But whose legacy cast a shadow
Over the eternal daytime.

A woman I never knew,
But whose broken soul,
Fractured by a broken home,
Shattered mine and others long
Before our stories began.

A woman I never knew,
Moulded in a loveless game,
Where rot and decay took
The place of family portraits

On walls littered with the
Fragrances of hate and betrayal,
In the presence of lustful minds,
Bastard offspring, and wounds that
Could never heal.

A woman I never knew,
Save the one time I
Have no memory of,
And perhaps for good
Reason, in a parliament
Where ill-articulated reason
Has often been seen as treason.

A woman I never knew,
Who held the position
Another wished to,
Another whose world was
Cremated by the painful happenstance
That succession induced.

A woman I never knew,
Whose blood runs through
These poisoned veins of a
Flock torn apart,
Never to know peace and
Reconciliation.

Farewell, to the woman I never knew.

END OF THE LINE?

Bloodlines are flowing,
Spawning generations new,
And they are close,
And aging already.

Those who came before
Grow further away,
With each new passing day.

Stories unwritten have flowed
Through time, legacies left behind.
Stories unwritten, but lived,
Have left their mark.

New stories, yet to be told,
But soon to begin,
Are upon us.

But not from me.

A legacy, a lineage, a story.

A weight upon the shoulders
Of every man
Who feels his ancestors
Towering over him,
Watching closely,
For what, and who,
Comes next.

This has continued,
But not as it should,
Not in truth.
This line is under threat.

With all that has come before,
With all who have gone before,
There may simply be no more.

Questions of morality,
Responsibility,
Choice.

But one question above all...

Is this the end of the line?

Printed in Dunstable, United Kingdom